D0874169

S O U T H W E S T E R N   S T U D I E S

MONOGRAPH No. 54

Antislavery in the Southwest

William G. Kephart's Mission to New Mexico, 1850-53

by

LAWRENCE R. MURPHY

TEXAS WESTERN PRESS
THE UNIVERSITY OF TEXAS AT EL PASO

ISBN 0-87407-112-0

ABOUT THE AUTHOR

Lawrence Richard Murphy, born in Sacramento on October 4, 1942, was reared in California. He attended the University of Arizona from which he received his baccalaureate and master's degrees in 1964-65; Texas Christian University awarded him the Ph.D. in 1968. His advanced work in Middle East history was at the American University in Cairo, Egypt in 1971-73. He has written and edited several books on New Mexico and the Southwest, including *Frontier Crusader — William F. M. Arny* (University of Arizona Press, 1972) and *Philmont: A History of New Mexico's Cimarron Country* (University of New Mexico Press, 1972). He was given the Best Southwestern Biography Award by the Border Regional Library Association in 1972. Now an Associate Professor of History at Western Illinois University, he makes his home in Macomb, Illinois.

182461

Antislavery in the Southwest: William G. Kephart's Mission to New Mexico 1850-1853

by

Lawrence R. Murphy

The year 1850 inaugurated a decade during which the United States moved slowly, almost imperceptably, yet inevitably, toward Civil War. Arguments over slavery grew increasingly passionate. For years, northern opposition to the "peculiar institution" had been growing; Southerners had developed an elaborate defense of their system of forced labor. Now a new element had clouded the already tense environment. In 1846 the United States went to war with Mexico amid cries that it was the nation's "manifest destiny" to expand to the Pacific. Within two years the war had been won and a large portion of northern Mexico had been annexed. Debate now centered on whether slavery should be allowed to spread into the newly-acquired regions.

The two critical issues of the era — expansion and slavery — first united in the Territory of New Mexico. Such political leaders as New Englander Daniel Webster believed that because a plantation economy could never expand into such an area, there was no reason to worry about slavery extending into the region.[1] Northern antislavery leaders were less confident, however, and worked diligently to exclude slavery from the Southwest. It is the story of their efforts upon which this study focuses.

"Our committee must soon do something in relation to New Mexico," wrote the Reverend George Whipple, secretary of the American Missionary Association in February 1850. Founded at Albany, New York four years before, Whipple's group sent Protestant missionaries to both American and foreign fields in the years before the

[3]

Civil War. Later, during the Reconstruction era, its major emphasis was on aiding freed Negroes in the South.[2] His letter was addressed to Arthur Tappan, a New York businessman and an active supporter of the missionary work. More importantly, Tappan was an abolitionist who had helped to found the American and Foreign Antislavery Society, one of the most potent abolitionist groups in America. Whipple and Tappan agreed that only by sending someone to New Mexico could the doctrines of Protestant Christianity and antislavery be planted on the new Southwest frontier. The prospects for taking immediate action seemed excellent. Whipple reported that already two donors had pledged $150 to support the project. He also knew someone to head up the work: William G. Kephart, a Free Presbyterian minister from Ripley, Ohio. In addition to being a good Christian and a dedicated abolitionist, Kephart had enough experience as a printer to set up an antislavery press in the Southwest. "He appears to be a man of mind and judgment. His principles are firm; whether his piety is as deep, I have not the opportunity of judging," noted Whipple. "All I know of him is favorable." Simeon S. Jocelyn, another abolitionist leader, also "thought well of the appointment," although expressing concern about Kephart's desire to establish Free Presbyterian churches. "Let the pure gospel be preached," he concluded, "and churches be formed as may be."[3]

These succinct characterizations constitute most of what is known about Kephart, a man whose entire life seems to have been shrouded in obscurity. Kephart's birthdate is even uncertain, although likely he was in his early thirties by midcentury.[4] Most of his life had been spent in Ripley, a small Ohio River town fifty miles below Cincinnati and a hotbed of antislavery sentiment. Runaway slaves often found ready shelter in the town or on nearby farms after escaping across the Ohio.[5]

The central figure in this abolitionist ferment and Kephart's mentor was the Rev. John Rankin. A Tennessee native, Rankin began preaching at Carlisle, Kentucky in 1819. Converted to abolitionism by Charles G. Finney, he moved across the Ohio to Ripley four years later. A series of letters written to condemn his own brother's purchase of slaves established him as a major abolitionist in the Northwest. His 1833 volume of *Letters on American Slavery* rejected the concept of white supremacy and argued that the oppressive system of slavery prevented blacks from developing their talents fully. The American Antislavery Society had been sufficiently impressed with Rankin that it hired him to travel throughout the Northwest promoting abolitionism.[6]

Beginning in 1822 Rankin pastored the Ripley Presbyterian Church, gathering around him a number of youthful disciples such as Kephart. By the early 1840s, Rankin discovered that his own church was at odds with other Presbyterians over the issue of slavery. The local congregation banned slaveowners from its membership, for example, only to be overruled by the Presbyterian General Assembly. When the Assembly refused to suspend a minister who supported slavery, Ripley churchmen favored separating from the denomination. Other similarly-minded Presbyterians also seceded, and eventually sixty-five churches from Pennsylvania to Iowa banded together as "Free Presbyterians."[7]

Having grown up in such an environment, young Kephart seemed ideal to lead an antislavery mission to New Mexico. The American and Foreign Antislavery Society joined Whipple's American Missionary Association in paying Kephart's travel costs and living expenses. He was to distribute tracts, to "show the inhabitants the advantages of free over slave labor, to promote education and the formation of sabbath schools and a church, to encourage the establishment of a free press, to communicate to the Committee valuable information, . . . and to preach the gospel."[8]

Kephart left a detailed record of his work in New Mexico. Letters sent to Whipple at least once a month and often every week described his religious activities. He commented extensively on social and political matters as well. Sometimes Whipple edited these for publication in the organization's monthly *American Missionary*. On antislavery matters, Kephart occasionally wrote Arthur Tappan, but more often his reports were directed to Dr. Gamaliel Bailey, editor of the *National Era*, a leading abolitionist weekly published in the nation's capital. These received wide circulation and were often reprinted in other journals.[9] Kephart also wrote a few letters, mostly

William G. Kephart

John T. Rankin

during the early months of his work, to the *Ripley Bee*, a local weekly edited by his brother-in-law, Charles F. Campbell,[10] to the *Free Presbyterian*, a church paper, and to Horace Greeley's *New York Tribune*.[11]

Kephart worked in New Mexico from mid-November 1850 until February 1853. In addition to distributing abolitionist materials and working to establish a church, he helped found and for a time edited the *Santa Fe Weekly Gazette*, a pioneer New Mexico paper. It became increasingly evident that Kephart was the wrong man to spread Christianity and antislavery in the Southwest. He was unable to speak Spanish and thus could not communicate with most of the people. His complete lack of understanding or sympathy for the local customs of New Mexico's Mexican-American population undermined his position in the territory. His special aptitude for making enemies further reduced his possible influence.

What finally led to Kephart's removal was not his failure as a preacher or abolitionist so much as the amount of money he was spending. At first, expenditures for food, clothing, and a rented room had been quite moderate. Costs increased rapidly, however, after he took over the unprofitable *Gazette*. The paper lost so much money that first Kephart asked Whipple for $500, and nearly every subsequent letter asked for more. In all, his expenditures totalled over $6,500, of which the missionary group paid some $2,300. The remainder came from the antislavery society and individual donors.[12] As important as New Mexico might have seemed three years before, too many other areas existed where money could be better spent in 1853.

By the time that the decision was made to close the New Mexico mission, Kephart had already left the Southwest. Apparently apprehensive over Whipple's displeasure with his high expenses and unauthorized drafts, the *Gazette*'s editor announced his forthcoming departure for the States late in January 1853. Kephart gave every indication that he intended to return and promised to send back frequent reports for publication in the paper. He may well have sensed that his work was over, however, for he wrote a lengthy farewell letter "to our readers."[13]

Kephart's departure from New Mexico enabled him to make one last appeal that his missionary and abolitionist work be continued. Crossing the plains by almost the same route that had brought him West three years before, he reached Washington early enough in March to attend the inauguration of President Franklin Pierce.[14] His real reason for visiting the capital was to plead his case personally before Whipple and other leaders of the societies which had sent him. Kephart argued that he or someone else should be returned to New Mexico.[15] Apparently no final decision was reached before his return via Philadelphia and New York to Ripley in May. Not until June 30, 1853, did he learn officially of the committee's final decision to abandon the New Mexico work.[16]

News traveled slowly, and it was November before *Gazette* editor James L. Collins found his former associate listed as editor of the *Free Presbyterian.* Complaining that Kephart had given "poor and insufficient reason" for not coming back, Collins reprinted Kephart's inaugural statement upon taking up the editorship of the *Presbyterian.* In it Kephart noted that his "first choice and most ardent desire was to return to my former field of labor in New Mexico." "Dark and unpromising as that field was," he added, "yet more than two years of labor in it had won for it my strongest sympathy, and I would willing[ly] have consecrated for the good of her people what little zeal and ability I could command, for the remainder of my days, had such seemed the indication of Providence."[17]

Kephart remained in Ohio working with the Free Presbyterian church for the rest of the decade. Besides his work with the church's paper, he served as pastor at Porter, a small town ten miles north of the Ohio River. He was active in church affairs, delivering the opening sermon at the synod's 1856 meeting and moderating at the annual conference two years later. When the church established a new weekly publication, *The Free Church Portfolio,* Kephart was named a corresponding editor.[18] The outbreak of the Civil War took him into the army as a chaplain with the Tenth Iowa regiment.[19]

With peace restored and many antislavery principles established as national policy, Kephart returned to the West. He pastored churches in Atlantic, Iowa, and Cheyenne, Wyoming, again facing the challenge of Christianizing frontier societies. His final assignment was as a missionary in South Dakota. Forced to retire from active preaching because of failing eyesight, Kephart returned to the Southwest after a twenty-year absence. His last years were spent with a daughter, Mrs. Mary K. King, at Deming, New Mexico, where he died May 29, 1894.[20]

What then was the significance of William G. Kephart's unsuccessful antislavery activities in New Mexico? First, his voluminous correspondence provides a detailed, although highly subjective, view of New Mexico Territory during its formative years. Only the recently published diary of Governor David Meriwether and the army letters of Colonel George A. McCall[21] contain anything like Kephart's intimate view of the Southwest in the early 1850s. Second, and perhaps more important on the national level, the failure of Kephart's campaign demonstrated how irrelevant the issue of slavery was to those who lived in the Mexican cession. The fears of the abolitionists were unfounded. Even when the Civil War reached New Mexico, most Southwesterners were more concerned about an invasion from their traditional enemies in Texas than about the danger of slavery expanding into their homeland. Finally, Kephart was perhaps typical of the individuals who lead reform movements. While steadfastly opposing the enslavement of blacks, he demonstrated his own prejudices toward Mexican-Americans and Catholics. He was so convinced of the rightness of his cause and the importance of his crusade that he could not accept the viewpoints of others or recognize their accomplishments. This stubbornness, prejudice, and inability to adjust to the conditions of the Southwest caused the eventual and inevitable failure of William G. Kephart's New Mexico mission.

The Trail to Santa Fe

Americans had been traversing the Great Plains between Missouri and New Mexico for nearly three decades by the time young William Kephart reached Independence in early September 1850. Such pioneers as William Becknell had been followed by hundreds of other merchants. The trade was profitable, and the value of goods carried west gradually increased. The dangers of western travel had diminished (although not entirely disappeared) as routes became better known, water and forage locations were mapped, treaties were negotiated with Indian tribes, and military escorts were provided to protect caravans.[22]

As settlement pushed westward, what had been wild frontier towns on the edge of the settlement became increasingly civilized. "But a few years since," Kephart explained in his first letter to the *National Era,* "a trip to St. Louis was associated with all the border tales of bold adventure, with a voyage to India, or the circumnavigation of the globe." Now, however, with the American empire expanding steadily into the West, St. Louis was a "vast city — vast in its rapidly increasing population — vast in its resources — vast in its future destinies — a mighty commercial heart, throbbing with a healthful vitality." Even Independence, an outpost town from which travelers departed for the far west, had a permanent population of 2,000; thousands more funneled through on their ways to Utah, California, or New Mexico.[23]

Kephart arrived in the West at a moment of especially rapid development. Gold had been discovered in California two years before, and thousands of would-be prospectors were heading for the Mother Lode country. "Our town is yet quite crowded with emigrants," a newspaper correspondent in Independence reported in mid-May; "the numbers passing through greatly exceeded our expectation." He predicted the number would exceed the previous year's record of 8,000 by nearly a third.[24]

The Treaty of Guadalupe-Hidalgo, which formalized New Mexico's annexation to the United States, was only two years old, and other Americans were bound for Santa Fe to take advantage of new opportunities which had opened up there. The number of trading caravans departing for the Southwest had grown steadily. Dr. Henry Connelley (later New Mexico's Civil War governor), the famed trader Francis X. Aubry, and William Bent, brother of the assassinated New Mexico governor, were only three of the many traders who crossed the plains in 1850.[25] To satisfy the need for improved communication with the Southwest, the United States government contracted for monthly mail service from Missouri to Santa Fe with the firm of Waldo, Hall and Company. The first of their new, color-fully painted, watertight stages departed Independence July 1, 1850.[26] Soldiers were needed in the West to erect forts along the trail, tame the Indians, or prevent renewed Mexican-Americans re-sistance to United States occupation. In mid-July 1850 some four hundred dragoon and infantry soldiers left Fort Leavenworth, just west of Independence, for Santa Fe. They were followed during the summer and early fall by several other large contingents. To transport government freight across the plains, on September 4, the day after Kephart reached Independence, the firm of Judge James Brown, William H. Russell (later a partner in the legendary Russell, Majors and Waddell) and John S. Jones contracted with the army to haul 600,000 pounds of freight from Ft. Leavenworth to Santa Fe for 14-1/3 cents per pound.[27]

Kephart soon discovered that despite such improvement, the West could still be exciting. At 2:00 o'clock one morning in Inde-pendence a building filled with ammunition caught fire. Exploding powder blew the structure "to atoms, shaking the earth for several miles around like the ground swell of an earthquake." More serious-ly, the mail from Santa Fe brought the frightening news that Indians on the plains had been attacking soldiers and Mexican hunters. Sev-eral had been killed.[28]

Kephart's fascination with the frontier and his imminent depar-ture into the wilderness did not dull his interest in politics — espe-cially related to slavery. For several months Congress had been de-bating the future of the area acquired from Mexico. Kephart learn-ed in Independence that legislation had been passed extending the Texas boundary to include land traditionally claimed by New Mex-ico. He was appalled by the news, which others interpreted as a reasonable compromise: "plying the timid with the lash and the mercenary with Texas scrip," he claimed with typically exaggerated rhetoric, slave owners had persuaded Congress to "dismember New Mexico of millions of acres in derogation of all right, hand it over to marauding Texans to be converted into slave territory, and pa-triotically pay her a bonus of ten millions to take it." He correctly predicted that soon Congress would enact a new fugitive slave act making it more difficult for blacks to escape from bondage.[29]

Kephart may not have heard before he left for New Mexico that on September 9, 1850 (while he was still in Independence), legislation had been signed admitting New Mexico as a territory. Accepting Stephen A. Douglas' contention that westerners should be allowed to make their own decisions regarding important political questions, the act allowed New Mexico (and Utah) to exercise "squatter sovereignty" and decide for itself whether to allow slavery or not. Kephart now had a major new task: make certain that the people of New Mexico excluded slaves.

Kephart's travels through Missouri and Kansas had demonstrated the importance of his work by showing how easily a free area could be changed into a slave one. Kansas was "fast filling with whites," a majority of whom seemed to have slaves. Every family Kephart saw had "domestics" with them. Already, too, there was talk of opening up new Indian lands for settlement, and Kephart was certain that before this happened "slavery will have fixed its relentless grasp upon it, and will claim it by right of preoccupation; and then there will be another compromise, in which slavery will get all she asks."[30] The same thing must not occur in New Mexico.

Kephart became interested in the uniquely western problem of Indian relations. His reaction hinted that his seeming compassion for slaves might not be transferable to other minorities. After only a few days in the West and conversations with a handful of inhabitants, he concluded that the government's policy was wrong and had to be changed before the Indians could "be even *civilized*, much less *Christianized*." "Things are ripening fast here already for a skirmish between the whites and the Indians," he reported, and "it need not surprise you, at any time to hear that blood has been shed in profusion." The whites did not see how violence could be avoided and complained of the government's ineffective policies. "The whites cheat the Indians, and the Indians, in turn, steal from the whites. This leads as a matter of necessity, to mutual jealousies and recriminations, which must ultimately end in an open rupture."

The essence of the problem, Kephart concluded, was that the

Indians had been allowed to keep *"too much land."* He was quick to prescribe treatment for the Indian problem. "If the Government would take an enumeration of all the Indians," he proposed, and "apportion to each family, or to each individual, as much land as would, by a proper cultivation, yield a competency; make each individual's possessions inalienable; confine them to their own possessions, and make them feel that they were to depend upon *that* resource for subsistence; and then extend over them a wholesome government — it would accomplish more for their civilization in ten years than . . . it has ever yet done in the whole history of our Indian treaties and Indian missions."[31] Years later the Dawes Severalty Act of 1887 enacted somewhat similar proposals that did not, as Kephart had predicted, solve the problems.

After a two-week delay, Kephart arranged to travel to New Mexico with Brown, Russell, and Company's first freight train, scheduled to leave Fort Leavenworth on September 14. "Tomorrow," he wrote, "we expect to hoist our canvas for a voyage over the plains." He explained that although using ox power and vehicles which were "not exactly in 'ship-shape,' " he found that canvass was an "indispensable article. I fancy a fleet of the line would not make a much more imposing appearance than we will." Kephart's train of thirty wagons carried nearly 150,000 pounds of government freight. It would not be alone, for a company of soldiers had left the day before and other wagons were preparing for departure. In a few weeks, Kephart predicted, "an almost unbroken chain of caravans" would stretch across the Plains, and even these would be insufficient to carry all the freight awaiting transport.

The first major stop along the trail was Council Grove, about 150 miles west of Independence. Named because an Osage Indian treaty has been signed there, these woods provided the last reliable source for lumber, water, and forage for wagon trains headed west. Kephart found a settlement of about 75 persons, the employees of Waldo, Hall, and Company, which had established a depot several months earlier and sent out a blacksmith and farmers to cut hay and watch livestock. Just before Kephart's arrival, the Rev. Allen T. Ward began construction of a Methodist Indian mission and manual labor school.³² Most of the residents were either unmarried men or those who had left their wives in Missouri. One Council Grove man told Kephart that in four years of marriage, he had spent only a year with his spouse. This was indeed the frontier, "surrounded by savages, and without the refining, humanizing influence of female association." There was hope, however, for most of the men regretted their situation and many lamented the absence of women. "How insatiate must be the lust of wealth," Kephart speculated, "that will reconcile men, even for a short time, to self-banishment from home and the refinements of civilized society, for no other purpose than the acquisition of a few paltry dollars."³³

From what had already happened at St. Louis, Independence, and Council Grove plus the vast amount of traffic on the trail, Kephart predicted that "in the course of a very few years, settlements of enterprising and adventurous whites will spring up as if by magic all along the line. They will gradually enlarge themselves into flourishing villages, and those villages in turn will be magnified into populous cities. The indolent and thriftless savage will melt away before the superior power and go-ahead enterprise of his white neighbor. The war-whoop will be superseded by the solemn church-bell, and the patient pack-mule and snail-paced ox-wagon will be run off the track by the snorting 'iron horse,' with his thundering train running a sweep-stake with the magnetic telegraph."³⁴

Kephart left Council Grove in early October and headed onto the Great Plains. The trip was so uneventful that few details were reported to Whipple or the *National Era*. For most of the trip, until he reached the crossing of the Dry Cimarron River in southwestern Kansas, Kephart traveled with the huge freight train. Then, to reach Santa Fe earlier than the slow wagons could make it, he and a traveler named McKensey went ahead with Judge James Brown on the latter's four-mule carriage. The prospect of traveling alone was still sufficiently dangerous that Kephart left his money with one of the wagon masters with instructions to return it to Whipple should he be captured or killed. "I did this merely to guard against a *possible* contingency," he explained later, "and not that I had any serious apprehension of danger, for I have felt from the first that the Lord had work for me to do *here,* and that He would carry me safely through every peril, to my destined field." Brown drove "as if his mules had been trained in the Hippodrome of Bonn," and the party soon caught up with another train with which they stayed nearly to Santa Fe.

Caravans sought to reach New Mexico early enough in the fall to avoid being caught in a storm. Kephart had left unusually late and encountered an early blizzard the first week in November. "A snowstorm on the plains!" he later explained. "You who live in the states have no conception of the terror which it inspires in the breasts of those who are crossing the plains at this season. Scarcely did Elijah from the summit of Carmel watch with deeper interest the gathering clouds than do these way-farers of the plains watch the varied shades and tints of sunset. . . ." Fortunately, the storm lasted only three days, and because of warm temperatures left only six inches of snow on the ground.[35]

"After a protracted journey of two months" Kephart arrived in New Mexico's capital November 17, 1850. He was, in his own words, "in 'good order and well conditioned' for one who had been an out-cast from civilization, wandering over 'wide-extended plains' and 'cloud-capped' mountains" for so long. Now he could begin the work for which he had come, introducing Protestantism and abolitionism to the people of New Mexico.[36]

At first Kephart found lodging in Santa Fe with Indian Superintendent James S. Calhoun, a Georgia gentleman soon to be named the territory's first governor. For a more permanent arrangement, he rented a house with the Rev. Enoch Nicholson, a Methodist missionary who had arrived in New Mexico just a few days before him. The building contained one large room where chapel services were to be held, another for a study and book shop, and living accommodations for Nicholson, his wife, and Kephart. A large sign painted with a protestant flag hung outside to announce their presence.[37]

"Sodom and Gomorrah"

Kephart's initial impressions of Santa Fe were largely negative, in part because of his own cultural intolerance, also because of the crudeness which sometimes seemed to dominate New Mexico during the first years of American rule. No doubt Kephart, like other missionaries, realized that his own work could be better justified if he exaggerated the conditions he found. Society on the frontier was frequently violent, with several "atrocious murders" reported during the winter of 1850-51. One of the killers, Kephart thought, would be hung "unless he can bribe his keepers, and make his escape."

Kephart blamed the gambling halls and fandango rooms for the high crime rate. Thousands, even hundreds of thousands, of dollars, he reported, were annually "swallowed up" in these "maelstroms of dissipation and ruin." The previous year a wagon master employed by Judge Brown's company "threw himself in the stream of dissipation, and was soon borne upon the rocks, and ruined." He sold the goods in his charge to pay gambling debts and eventually fled to California owing his employer $10,000.[38]

Sexual standards were "the most deplorable that could be conceived," so bad that Kephart labeled New Mexico as "sodom and gomorrah viewed through a microscope." Prostitution was so common that it seemed "almost universal among Mexican women." Kephart admitted that there probably were "a few virtuous women," although prostitution was the rule and chastity the exception. "It is painful," he explained, "to see to what a profound degradation human nature can sink itself when left to the freedom of its own will" and difficult to imagine that these "sunken and debased" women could ever be redeemed.

Adopting anti-Catholic prejudices common at the time, Kephart blamed the Roman church for the immorality he found. He had heard rumors that the local priest had five mistresses and that the clergy throughout the territory kept women. "Among a population who have been accustomed for generations to look upon such men as their spiritual guides and examples, enpowered of Heaven to forgive their sins," Kephart asked, "is it marvelous that prostitution should have been universal or that fathers and mothers should be found selling their own daughters . . .?" Because licentiousness was sustained by public opinion and encouraged by respected churchmen, however, it would be unfair to condemn these women as in the States. "Let the American mothers and daughters, then, pity rather than execrate these unfortunate ones, remembering . . . [that] the compassionate Son of God said: 'Daughter, go thy way, sin no more.' "39

Americans had an obligation to be "models of perfection" in the Southwest. "Scarcely could a slave on a southern plantation," Kephart analogized in terms his abolitionist readers could well understand, "manifest more abjectness of demeanor toward his master, than do these Mexicans toward an American. They look up to us as a superior race." Kephart concluded that the only hope for New Mexico was that Americans would "renovate this land, dissipate its night of ignorance and depredation, and fill it with the light of civilization and [Protestant] Christianity." Unfortunately, however, most Americans who had come to the Southwest set such bad examples that they perpetuated "the state of things they ought to reform." Even one minister "became more famous at the Monte-bank and fandango room than in the pulpit." His behavior so outraged the community that he escaped being tarred and feathered only by fleeing to California.40

Despite the "dark moral picture" he painted, Kephart was hopeful that New Mexico could be improved. The people showed many "redeeming traits of character." "There is a natural ease and gracefulness of deportment," he explained, "blended with filthy rags and marks of deepest abjection." Mexican-Americans were extremely urbane, equalled only by Frenchmen and far transcending Americans. "They are sympathetic and impulsive in their feelings," he added, noting that "in this lies the element of their ruin." Kephart's prescription for curing New Mexico's seeming illnesses were easy, reflecting both his inclination toward simplistic solutions and the ethno-centrism which infected his generation. "In short, if this people could be Americanized, and receive the polish and refinement of education and civilization, and above all the chastening, purifying influence of our holy religion, they would become a most interesting part of our population."41

Starting a Protestant Church

The home missionary movement in the United States found the Mexican Cession a particularly attractive place to which to send workers in the years immediately following the War with Mexico. Most religious workers went to California or Oregon, where the possibilities seemed more hopeful.[42] Kephart was not alone in attempting to introduce American-style protestantism to the Mexican Catholics of the Southwest, however, for the Methodists and Baptists had also assigned clergy to Santa Fe by 1850.

Rev. Hiram W. Read was one of the first protestant preachers to arrive in New Mexico. Kephart's earliest reports on Read showed that his intolerance to Indians, Mexican-Americans, and Catholics extended even to his co-religionists. Read was a Baptist, Kephart told his superiors, and following the rules of his church had refused for two years to celebrate communion for the "few faithful ones" in Santa Fe because they had not been immersed. Read had been, in Kephart's view, "grossly negligent" in denying the sacrament to men and women "whose souls panted for the blessed privilege of communing at the table of their Lord." Moreover, Read had served as a military chaplain, aligning himself too closely with what Kephart considered an essentially immoral institution. Kephart also interpreted Read's friendly approaches to him as conspiratorially motivated: Read's congregation had dwindled to a handful, and Kephart was certain that he was to be used to help "re-collect his audience."[43] With such condemnation as an overture, the two men refused to work together, never got along, and Kephart used every opportunity to condemn Read, although he did discourage Whipple from printing any of the details.

More cordial relationships developed with Reverend Enoch Nicholson, the first representative of the Methodist Church, North, sent to New Mexico.[44] The two clergymen lived together, shared expenses, and began conducting joint Sunday services soon after their arrival. November 17, 1850, they offered the first Protestant sacrament in New Mexico, after which Kephart preached his inaugural sermon on "the Christian's privilege and assurance in view of the

character of his great high priest." That afternoon a few children attended their sabbath school, and come evening Kephart preached at the army's candlelight service.[45]

Both Kephart and Nicholson shared a hatred of Catholics. In addition to condemning priestly immorality, they distributed anti-Catholic tracts brought from the states. Nicholson created a considerable stir by circulating a pamphlet which denied Mary's perpetual virginity by discussing her children other than Jesus. "The priest," Kephart reported, "denounced the doctrine [as] heretical, and the poor, little book, was, of course, Anethema." Other publications denounced the Papacy and condemned the Roman church for charging fees for baptisms, marriages, and burials.[46] The two Protestants persisted in circulating their inflamatory booklets, arguing that "the people will read them, the vicario and Priests to the contrary notwithstanding."[47]

Kephart hoped to increase his effectiveness by preaching in the haunts of the sinners. Late in January, 1851, he arranged to speak in the billiard room of the Exchange Hotel, which he identified as "the most extensive gambling house I ever saw." According to historian Ralph W. Twitchell, the hostelry, more familiarly known as La Fonda (the Inn), had gambling tables which "lured the prospectors, soldiers, traders, trappers, and mountaineers for miles around, and its liquid cheer soon gave to the tenderfoot sojourner all the courage, dash, and dare-devil spirit of the true son of the desert."[48] The "motley assemblage" which had gathered by 3:00 to hear Kephart's sermon about the Prodigal son listened with "great attention" and eagerly sought the tracts he offered afterward. "I believe the Lord will bless that sermon," Kephart wrote Whipple, "and the tracts, and make them productive of good."[49]

Kephart realized his limitations in conducting religious work. Some materials specifically related to the evils of gambling and some illustrations showing the ill effect of alcohol on the stomach would make his sermons more effective. More serious, because he spoke no Spanish, he was unable to reach most New Mexicans. He requested some language books to study and suggested that the American Missionary Association consider employing a Spanish-speaking preacher to assist him. "A man who can talk Spanish fluent-ly," he admitted, "possesses a great influence over the population, while one who cannot speak it at all, or who speaks it badly, can have but little or no influence at all over them."[50]

Promoting Abolitionism

In addition to observing conditions in New Mexico and preach-ing the Protestant gospel, Kephart's assignment included persuad-ing New Mexicans to exclude slaves from the territory. To accom-plish this objective he brought with him a large supply of tracts de-signed to influence public opinion.

William Jay, son of the first Chief Justice of the United States, John Jay, had written the most important, and "Address to the In-habitants of New Mexico and California." Young Jay was a pro-minent New York abolitionist who had worked with William Lloyd Garrison, helped found several antislavery organizations, and auth-ored a number of antislavery tracts.[51] The "Address," which had been written in August 1849, warned residents of the Mexican Ces-sion of the educational, industrial, religious, moral, legal, and mil-itary backwardness of the slave states, and condemned the national government for having failed to establish territorial governments in the West. "Let no feudal lord with his serfs come among you to rob you of your equal share of the rich deposits of your soil," he warned the frontiersmen. "Tolerate no servile cast, kept in ignor-ance and degradation to minister to the power and wealth of an oppressive aristocracy." Jay urged the territories to declare them-selves independent of American rule "unless exempted from the curses of slavery" and promised the support of the North for such an endeavor. "Up," he concluded, "quit yourselves like men, and may the favor of God and the blessings of generations come to rest upon you."[52]

Despite the fact that many of Jay's arguments were out-of-date as a result of Congressional action awarding statehood to California and creating New Mexico Territory, as soon as he arrived in Santa Fe, Kephart had copies of the booklet printed in Spanish and began to consider ways of distributing it as widely as possible. At first he hoped to work through the Catholic clergy. He would give copies to the Santa Fe priest to distribute and secure letters of commendation from him which would enable him to gain the assistance of the priests in smaller towns. Everything would be done secretly "so as not to arouse the vigilance of the opposition. If I can have the priests on my side, and God's approbation of the work," Kephart was sure the effort would be successful.[53] The more his anti-Catholicism intensified, however, the less workable the scheme seemed. After all, Kephart concluded, since the Jay tract included a chapter on the evils of ignorance, priests who wanted to keep their people unschooled would be unlikely to circulate it.[54]

As an alternative, Kephart hired a Mexican-American, formerly the sheriff of Santa Fe, who claimed to know everyone who could read and who was willing to distribute both religious booklets and the Jay "Address." He circulated about forty-five copies one evening. Apparently during the night some New Mexico politicians obtained copies, read the booklet, found its arguments objectionable, and the next morning threatened the man with violence if any more were distributed. "There has been a great ferment in the community or at least among a certain class of [the] community since." The Reverend Nicholson, who received warnings not to associate too closely with Kephart, suggested the two preachers "amicably separate." Kephart blamed the Methodist board, rather than Nicholson, since its instructions prohibited preachers from involving themselves in political controversy. "So our separation is complete. He has made his election," Kephart lamented, "and avows his policy to be the say-nothing-on-the-subject policy." Kephart himself vowed to continue "speaking for the church, though I should die for it on the streets of Santa Fe."

To determine for himself whether it was wise to continue circulating the "Address," Kephart submitted copies to army commander Colonel James S. Monroe, Judge Joab Houghton, Senator-elect Hugh N. Smith, and Prosecuting Attorney Merrill Ashurst, asking each if the document contained anything contrary to the United States constitution or territorial laws and whether it was likely to *"incite insurrection"* among the Mexican-American population. All agreed that the booklet contained nothing *"illegal,"* however, they unanimously argued that it would have "a pernicious effect" if circulated and should be withdrawn. For one thing, the tract accused the United States government of "bad faith" toward New Mexico, a true enough statement only partially alleviated by the subsequent creation of New Mexico Territory. Such accusations would be hard to deny and might further "sour the Mexican feeling against the government." More serious, the "Address" assured New Mexicans that "they *have themselves all the elements of a great empire,* [and] exhorts them in a certain contingency to strike for independence." Kephart explained to Whipple why he now appreciated the danger of such statements: "These people entertain toward our government the same feeling *always* possessed by a *conquered* people toward their *conquerors*. They would throw off the yoke at any time, and set up for themselves if they thought it would be practical." The problems became more serious because so many people who could not read would depend on rumor and exaggerated impressions. "Those who read the Address," he continued, "catching most likely a false impression, will take it as an appeal to them to strike for independence, with the assurance that the North will aid them in such a struggle." Others eager to secure plunder would join any revolutionary alliance promising booty. The result could be "a formidable, and most sanguinary insurrection in the midst of us, with indiscriminate havoc." The suggestion that abolitionists were encouraging insurrection, with the "Address" as evidence, was likely to hurt the antislavery cause.

Despite his admission that the "Address" could have disruptive influence among the Mexican-American population and his decision to withdraw it from circulation, Kephart believed that the strong reaction to it demonstrated the extent of pro-slavery sentiment in New Mexico. "The *controlling influences* here," he reported, "are pro-slavery, and almost the whole of the American population is from the slave states." Many Mexican-Americans were so "ignorant, and unprincipled, and as uncertain as the wind" that they could be easily won over by promises of financial reward. There was hope, however, demonstrated by the lack of racism among Mexican-Americans, many of whom were willing to associate with Negroes and even preferred them to white Americans.

Kephart tried to portray himself as a lone soldier fighting to save New Mexico from slavery. No one else would come to his aid; even those citizens with abolitionist feelings were unwilling to speak out openly. Kephart predicted that the enemy would use every means to "cripple" his efforts. He promised to do his best: "I rely upon the help of God to triumph over their avarice, and outride the storm of their violence." Help was needed urgently, though, and he urged eastern abolitionists to encourage others to come. If full-time workers could not be employed, then it might be possible to encourage antislavery men to come to New Mexico on their own. Grocerymen, mechanics, doctors, druggists, industrialists, farmers, lawyers, and other professionals were badly needed, he argued, and could make a good living in the Southwest. If only more "men of sterling integrity, decisive character, and pure in heart" could be found, the territory might yet be saved from slavery.[55]

Famous Men of New Mexico

Early in 1851, Kephart met the "world-renowned Kit Carson," already famous in the East through dime novels and other popular reports of his frontier exploits.[56] Kephart was surprised that Carson was not dressed in the "outlandish" costumes expected for hunters and trappers; he wore ordinary "genteel American costume," although Kephart was uncertain whether this was his customary attire. "Carson is rather under the medium height," Kephart reported, "but his frame is exceedingly well knit, muscular, and symetrically proportioned. His hair, a light auburn, and worn long, falls back from a forehead high, broad, and indicating more than a common share of intellect. The general contour of the face is not handsome, and yet not unpleasing. But that which at once arrests, and almost monopolizes, your attention is the eye; such an *eye!* gray, searching, *piercing,* as if with every glance he would reach the very wellsprings of thought, and read your very silent imaginings."

Kit Carson
[MUSEUM OF NEW MEXICO]

Kephart also met a friend of Carson's, less famous, but equally known and feared by all the Indians of the Southwest: John L. Hatcher, "a little taller" than Carson, "but more slenderly made, sandy hair, light, small blue eyes, keen in their glance, slightly inclining to a squint, and continually dancing and flashing about, as if all the time looking out for a Navahoe or an Apache. His glance is quick and piercing, but not steady and penetrating like that of Carson. His face and head are rather small than otherwise, and do not indicate as much intellectuality as Kit's. His movements are of the most mercurial kind, so that you are not long in making up your mind to the verdict that if *caught,* it will not be napping."[57]

While Kephart seemed infatuated with these frontiersmen, he found little good to say about John R. Bartlett, another famous American in the Southwest. The two men never met, but Kephart learned from an "authentic source" that Bartlett had been named to head a United States commission to survey the southern boundary of the Mexican Cession. Late in January, 1851, bands of robbers and murderers were rampaging through the settlements of Socorro and San Elizario near El Paso. "Houses were opened," reported Bartlett, "for the indulgence of every wicked passion; and each midnight hour heralded new violent and often bloody scenes for the fast filling record of crime." Bartlett sent out possees from his survey party to round up the accused murderers, swiftly tried them, and executed those found guilty as soon as half an hour after their conviction. Bartlett was proud of what he had done,[58] but Kephart was appalled by his action: "what strikes us as a *little peculiar,*" he reported, "is, that a *Boundary Commissioner* and his assistants *should constitute* themselves high court of life and death in a case which clearly came within the range of the civil jurisdiction." Perhaps this was a new and strange example of 'progressive democracy.' "[59]

Late in March, Kephart heard reports that a new Catholic Bishop assigned to Santa Fe was en route from the east. Leading Mexican Catholics would welcome his arrival, since they were "dissatisfied with the present state of things in their church." He correctly predicted that many of the clergy would oppose his coming. Kephart assumed that since the churchman came from Louisville, he no

Archbishop Jean B. Lamy
[HISTORICAL SOCIETY OF N. M.]

doubt favored slavery. In a statement which revealed how far he would stretch the facts to support his conspiratorial theories, Kephart argued that "the appointment of a bishop from the States for New Mexico" was "one link of a grand chain of pro-slavery measures designed to prepare the way for introducing slavery into this Territory."[60]

Bishop Jean B. Lamy reached Santa Fe August 9, 1851. Kephart reported that he was received with a demonstration "something like what we might expect on the entrance of a triumphal warrior." The sound of exploding artillery summoned Kephart from his office to see the procession moving up a street leading to the church. "The street was spanned at intervals with richly embroidered shawls . . . reaching from house-top to house-top." A looking glass hung from the center of each. Some householders had brought cedar trees from the mountains and planted them in front of their homes for the day. In the official carriage, which led the parade, rode the territorial governor, James S. Calhoun, Bishop Lamy, and several other priests. Next came the two Baptist ministers, Read and the recently-arrived Reverend Smith. As usual Kephart took the opportunity to denounce Read for having "done about everything to compromise protestantism" and giving "public sanction to Romanism." That night the vicar gave a lavish banquet to welcome Lamy. Read attended, although Kephart and Nicholson declined to be present.[61]

Inaugurating the First Governor

From the moment he arrived in New Mexico, Kephart heard rumors about the appointment of the territory's first officials. Not until the arrival of the February mail did he and other Santa Feans learn that a man they already knew, James S. Calhoun, with whom Kephart had lived for a short time, had received the appointment. A Georgian who had served with President Zachary Taylor in the Mexican War, Calhoun had already spent twenty months in New Mexico as an Indian Agent.[62] Kephart was pleased with the selection, noting that it received "general approbation" in Santa Fe, "despite the chief executives' southern origins." "Governor Calhoun possesses many amiable qualities," he reported to the *National Era*, "and

James S. Calhoun
[MUSEUM OF NEW MEXICO]

though a southern man . . . , yet I think his first, and great aim here, in the Gubernatorial capacity, will be to try to bring *order* out of the *chaos* into which we have been plunged by the absence of any effective form of government."[63]

March 3, 1851, Kephart attended the inaugural ceremonies for the new governor. "This has been a great day for Santa Fe and New Mexico," he reported to his eastern friends, "with its concomitant explosions of gunpowder, champagne bottles, and patriotism." The ceremonies began at noon when a procession of dignitaries formed at the governor's residence. On a "spacious platform" which had been erected under the porch of the Governor's Palace, Chief Justice Joab Houghton administered the oath of office and read the President's commission proclaiming Calhoun as New Mexico Territorial Governor. Calhoun delivered an inaugural address in English; later it was translated into Spanish as well. "An era in the history of New Mexico commenced this day," he began.[64] Kephart described the speech as "of commendable length, delivered in a fervent and dignified manner."[65]

In what for him was exceptional praise, Kephart believed "no individual . . . could have been appointed with more general approbation." Calhoun was "gentlemanly, affable, dignified in his bearing, and commands general, perhaps I might say universal, respect and esteem." He had been an excellent Indian agent. Whether he would use his office to promote the extension of slavery into New Mexico, no one could predict. What he could contribute constructively was "the elevation and mental and moral improvement" of the new territory.

After the inaugural ceremonies were over, the "brazen-mouthed canons" on the plaza and smaller ones inside the Palace fired in salute. "A most copious outpouring of champagne followed." Kephart used the reception of which he wholeheartedly disapproved to attack the clergy. "It was perfectly astonishing to an unsophisticated tee-totaler," Kephart reported, "to see with what gusto the Romish ecclesiastics from the vicario down to the humble cura, guzzled down glass after glass of hot punch and sparkling champagne."

The procession then moved to the Catholic church for additional pageantry. Kephart's contempt for the procession was unbridled: "the grunting of horrible Latin," and the "confusion worse confounded of bass, tenor, alto, and soprano mixed in admirable discord, above which was heard the nerve lascerating squeals of an 'asthmatic' fiddle and pathsucking guitar." The procession returned to the palace where it adjourned to partake in additional libations.[66]

A Frightening Fire

March 21, 1851, fire broke out in the Exchange Hotel, the hostelry, gambling center, and saloon where Kephart had preached. The wooden structure was "wrapped in flames" within a few minutes. Little but the massive billiard tables (which were moved onto the adobe roof of an adjoining building) could be saved. A strong north wind rapidly spread the flames to adjacent buildings. Several were badly damaged, including the jewelry store of Spencer & Sabine. Santa Fe had no fire department, and little could be done to halt the flames. Not more than a dozen fire buckets, Kephart estimated, were used. At last the fire stopped "voluntarily, after it got among the adobes, as if it had become disgusted with such *dry pickings.*"

Kephart found it fascinating to watch adobe structures burn. "There is none of that wild leaping aloft of the flames, as if dancing in revelry over their wanton havoc. You see no pillars of fire standing over the tabernacle . . . ; but, *within* it is glowing like Nebuchadnezzar's furnace seven times heated." It was perfectly safe to walk on the roof until the timbers burned away or the mud roof became too hot. "There is a subterranean war beneath you; you are walking above a smothered volcano."

Kephart, with his usual exaggeration, supposed the fire would have political repercussions. The Mexican-Americans would see the catastrophe as "a special visitation from Heaven, sent in consequence of the Americans being in the country." This was the first major fire in Santa Fe's history, he explained, since before the arrival of the Americans, buildings had seldom been constructed of wood, and few houses contained enough flammable furniture to catch fire.

"This fire has taught us a lesson," he concluded, " . . . not to put up any more wooden houses here."[67]

Pioneer Editor

One of the reasons the American Missionary Association had picked Kephart for work in New Mexico was that his experience as a printer might enable him to open a Protestant, antislavery newspaper in the Southwest. The reception given Jay's "Address" convinced Kephart that materials written in the east were unsuitable for distribution in New Mexico. They were inevitably out-of-date and failed to consider local conditions. He proposed that the abolitionists buy a press and send out his brother-in-law from Ohio to edit a paper.[68] The high cost of such an endeavor apparently prevented the project from being initiated.

In fact New Mexico had already had several newspapers. The first, *The Santa Fe Republican,* had begun publication in September 1847 using equipment belonging to the United States army. It appeared intermittently, with the last known issue printed in August 1849. The first copy of a second paper, *The Santa Fe New Mexican,* was issued the following November, under the editorship of Edward T. Davies and William E. Jones. Only a few issues are known to exist before publication was suspended in May 1850.[69]

The third paper, *The Santa Fe Weekly Gazette,* has been described as "the first really successful newspaper in the territory." Established late in 1850 or early in 1851,[70] its principal owners were politician Hugh N. Smith, who doubtless hoped a newspaper could help him win political office, and trader James L. Collins, who probably provided most of the needed financing. According to Kephart, the paper encountered the same difficulties as its predecessors and almost failed twice during the first winter "for want of proper persons" to edit and publish it. When the latest printer left for the States in April, 1851, the owners approached Kephart and Nicholson to take charge. The two men laid down several conditions for assuming the editorial chair. Their own religious affiliations prohibited them from acting as the "organs of any political party or any individual." The paper must be "the vehicle of useful intelligence and an instrument of enlightening and elevating senses." The editors could not be controlled in what they printed. Correspondents might take whatever position they wanted, however, as long as the editors were not held responsible. Because religious issues were likely to dominate the forthcoming election campaign, the Protestant ministers preferred that their names not appear on the masthead until after the balloting. Kephart, recollecting the recent troubles over the "Address," also volunteered to refrain from commenting directly on the issue of slavery. The paper's owners considered these stipulations for several days.[71] Few printers or editors could be found in New Mexico, giving them no choice but to accept the offer or close down the paper. As a result of these conditions being accepted, Kephart's New Mexico mission changed directions dramatically. He no longer preached and seldom distributed tracts or undertook other religious activities. His antislavery efforts were largely limited to preparing lengthy letters for the *National Era*. Most of his time was devoted to editing and printing the weekly newspaper and conducting a job printing firm.

Nicholson apparently withdrew from the venture after a short time; in 1852 he returned to the states. The *Gazette*'s owners were sufficiently pleased with Kephart's work that in late June 1851, just before Collins left for the states, they asked him to become a partner in the enterprise. It seemed like an equitable offer: Kephart would be sold a third interest in the establishment for the nominal sum of $5 if he would edit and publish the paper and assume his share of future losses. "It does not at present pay expenses," he explained to Whipple, "but the owners think that with proper management, it can be made not only to do so, but to yield a profit as well." This arrangement was preferable to establishing a new abolitionist paper, since the *Gazette* was an established paper with a sizeable subscription list which could be conducted at little or no cost. Kephart even hoped to make enough to pay for printing tracts. Moreover, no new paper could be opened "without working up great hostility."[72] Henceforth, Kephart's name appeared as editor, and job printing was done by the company of "J. L. Collins & W. G. Kephart."[73]

Kephart soon became aware of the problems frontier editors faced.[74] Finances caused him constant worry. When Collins left for the states, he gave Kephart only $200 for expenses. An additional $7,000 or $8,000 in notes and accounts for collection were left with his Santa Fe agent, who was instructed to give the money to Kephart as it was needed. None could be collected, however, and Kephart was unable to secure payment for work he did. His only income came from a few subscriptions. His personal funds exhausted, the editor would have been unable to pay his employees had not the United States Marshall's office paid a $105 bill. "Last night," he lamented to Whipple, "I sat down almost with tears in my eyes to write Collins the real state of things and tell him that we could not *survive* much longer unless something were done on his part." Kephart soon received some additional money from Collins' agent, but he feared that unless the American Missionary Association or antislavery associations were willing to increase their contribution, the paper might suspend publication. "I should very much regret seeing the *Gazette* go down," he wrote, explaining that it was the only antislavery agency in New Mexico and "had done much to break the power of the priesthood here."[75]

Equally troublesome was the shortage of paper, type, and other printing materials. Kephart could earn a substantial profit, helping defray the newspaper's losses, by printing the annual laws and journals of the territorial legislature; but the old, worn-out type in the *Gazette* office was inadequate. Moreover, he hoped to begin the paper's second volume "in a new press and enlarged form, making our sheet large[r] and our type smaller." He was certain this "would make it look more like what a newspaper should be, and give room for a greater variety of material." Even before Kephart joined the firm, Collins had sent an order and the funds to pay for it to a St. Louis Company, but the list had failed to reach them. Collins took a second letter east with him. When the materials failed to reach Independence in time for the 1851 freighting season,[76] Kephart, eager to secure them as quickly as possible, hurriedly journeyed to Independence early the next spring. He procured the order and was back in Santa Fe by mid-April.[77]

Experienced printers were hard to find on the frontier, and once Kephart returned with the type, extra exertion was necessary to finish the legislative laws. "I have been up three nights in succession," he wrote Whipple in mid-summer, "working the press all night, and expect to work the greater part of every night for about three weeks to come." During the day all hands had been put to the tedious task of hand setting type. Kephart spent nights running off on the press what had been set during the day, so that the same type could be reused each day. When Collins contracted in Washington to print the journals of the two previous legislative sessions as well, Kephart concluded that "we shall have our hands full."[78]

The Maelstrom of New Mexico Politics

His insistence to the contrary notwithstanding, no sooner had Kephart assumed the editorial chair at the *Gazette* than he was thrust into the complex political wranglings which consumed the young territory. As the only newspaper in New Mexico, the *Gazette* could influence the outcome of elections; its columns could be used to praise or defame politicians. Moreover, its publishers sought lucrative territorial printing contracts and prepared broadsides and pamphlets for political uses. "I see not," Kephart explained to Whipple, "how I can move here at all effectively without having more or less to do with politics."[79] In fact Kephart became so well known for his partisan involvement that years later historian Ralph W. Twitchell identified him as "more of a politician than a missionary."[80]

As early as 1848, different reactions to the continuation of military rule in the territory stimulated the creation of two opposing parties. One group led by veteran trader James L. Collins and Attorney Joab Houghton preferred a territorial form of government, fearing that New Mexico might be admitted as a slave state. At an 1849 convention they chose Hugh N. Smith as a delegate to Congress on the presumption that New Mexico would be given territorial status. Smith and Collins had founded the *Gazette* to promote their political views. In opposition, trader Henry Connelly, former American Consul Manuel Alvarez, Indian Agent (later governor) James S.

Calhoun, and Washington office-seeker Major Richard H. Weightman advocated immediate statehood. To avoid the possibility that
Texas might annex all or part of New Mexico, they called a convention on May 15, 1850, framed a state constitution, and soon called
an election to chose officials. Their "legislature" chose Weighman
and Francis Cunningham as U.S. Senators. The *New Mexican* gen-
erally reflected their political views during its brief existence.[81]

While the creation of New Mexico territory erased the actions of
these extra-legal conventions, and both Smith and Weightman were
ultimately denied seats in Washington, factionalism persisted. At
first, Kephart remained aloof from politics. He found Calhoun personally attractive, and he was too occupied condemning immorality,
the Catholic church, and slavery to concern himself with partisan
questions. Gradually, however, he became a principal spokesman
for the Collins-Smith "independent party." At least officially it op-
posed the expansion of slavery into New Mexico, although more on
pragmatic than moral grounds, in contrast with the opposition faction that included many pro-slavery Southerners. Kephart especially liked Hugh Smith whom he considered the only true antislavery
man in the territory.[82] Perhaps more importantly, the Weightman
faction had close ties with the Catholic church. Kephart was appalled, for example, in April 1851 when the Governor's supporters nominated three priests for five positions in the territorial legislature.
"The coalition between the pro-slavery party and the Romish party,"
he concluded, "seems complete."[83] Kephart's employment by Collins
and Smith at the *Gazette* cemented an affiliation which had been
maturing for some time. "In my editorial courses," he reported after
several months as editor, "where it has been necessary to come into
contact with political questions (which is almost at every step), I
have usually taken sides with the Independent Party," since they
have "usually been in the right."[84]

The law under which New Mexico became a territory provided
that while the Governor, Secretary, and other officials were to be
nominated by the President and confirmed by the Senate, the citizens of the territory could elect the members of a territorial Council
and House of Representatives.[86] The first legislative election was

scheduled for late spring 1851. April 22 Kephart attended a caucus of the anti-Calhoun faction. Hugh Smith, who had been nominated as Territorial Secretary but not yet confirmed, gave the principal address. It was not uncommon for secretaries and governors to disagree, and Smith now attacked Governor Calhoun's administration as "ten-fold more oppressive and dictatorial" than the Mexican regime it had replaced. The meeting, being determined to beat the Governor's clique "at their own game," nominated a slate composed largely of Mexican-Americans and including several prominent Catholic clergymen. This bothered Kephart so much that he candidly admitted having "little sympathy" for either faction. Calhoun must be prevented from consolidating his power, however, and nearly any Mexican-American was more likely to oppose slavery than most Anglos.[86]

Politics heated up rapidly as election day neared. The Senate's refusal to confirm Smith, presumably as a result of Richard H. Weightman's opposition, set off another round of factional quarrelling. Smith's supporters held a public meeting to express their "disapprobation" at his rejection, and nominated him for a position in the territorial senate. Kephart admitted having "wrought considerably in politics" during the campaign. For him, religion, anti-slavery, and politics were closely associated. "I have no faith whatever in political parties or alliances in themselves considered or in their efficiency for accomplishing any good," he elaborated to Whipple, "only just so far as God may use them in his providence for furthering His own cause, and working out His own glory." He had "prayed for light and for the Spirit's guidance" and hoped that whatever impatience or combativeness he had shown could be forgiven. "Though sometimes I feel very much as though I were sailing between Scylla and Charybdis, yet I had rather die thus than to *rot* on a smooth sea in a dead calm."[87]

New Mexico's first territorial election "passed off with comparative quietness." Kephart objected to the amount of drunkenness and profanity, but was pleased that there was only one fight whereas on previous occasions the army had to be ordered out to put down riots. New Mexico society might be improving at last. The results were disappointing for the anti-Calhoun faction. Smith carried Santa Fe County by a large majority, but in San Miguel, where he had expected to win, the presence of the governor and alleged vote fraud resulted in his overall defeat. Attempts might now be made in Washington to prove that Smith was unpopular in the territory, but Kephart insisted that if "all *extraneous* influences" could be removed, he was still the most popular man in New Mexico.[88]

Just how little real power the legislature had became apparent during the first session. "The form of government which Congress has *inflicted upon us*," Kephart complained, "makes the Governor a dictator." Calhoun had manipulated the election by allowing non-New Mexico residents (Americans from the States) to vote and excluding the Pueblo Indians. His veto power over acts of the legislature was absolute. "Add to this enormous element of power the fact that almost all the appointment power for the territory is vested in the Executive, and that all the Indian agents are subject to his instructions . . . ," Kephart added, "and then tell me if I am mistaken in saying that our Executive is clothed with the powers of a dictator."[89] Calhoun further alienated Kephart by using his first annual message to call for the exclusion of Freedmen from New Mexico. "Free Negroes," he claimed "are regarded as nuisances in every State and Territory in the Union, and where they are tolerated, society is most depraved . . . . The disgusting degredation to which society is subjected by their presence, is obvious to all, and demands a prohibatory [sic] act of the severest nature."[90] Ironically, Kephart issued the Governor's speech as an extra of the *Gazette* and received the contract to print it as an eight-page pamphlet. However, he also issued an address from the opposition members of the legislature denouncing Calhoun and disclaiming responsibility for his unwise Indian policies.[91]

Each territory also elected a non-voting Delegate to the U.S. House of Representatives. When New Mexico held its first election in September 1851, the Calhoun faction nominated Richard H. Weightman, the army officer who had previously been refused a seat in the Senate. Kephart hoped that Hugh Smith would oppose him, but Captain A. W. Reynolds, another retired soldier, refused to withdraw his candidacy, and no one would challenge him at the party caucus. Kephart disliked Reynolds, a military man and a slave-owner, whom he considered "morally and mentally" unqualified for office. By now, however, Kephart was so involved in politics that he was willing to support Reynolds merely to "break down the Governor's faction."[92] After one of the most corrupt elections in New Mexico history, Weightman won by a majority of several hundred votes. Reynolds planned to contest the results in Washington, but Kephart preferred that neither man be seated. "It would teach the politicians here, as well as the people, a lesson that they will learn in no other way, and . . . would put a stop to these disgraceful frauds in the future."[93]

Weightman Versus Kephart

In New Mexico, Weightman suffered the disadvantage of not having a newspaper in which to argue his case or attack his opponents. No sooner had he reached Missouri en route to Washington, however, than he launched a strenuous conterattack aimed at strengthening his case in the capital. First in a letter published November 13, 1851, by the St. Louis *Missouri Republican,* later in correspondence to Senator Henry Foote of Mississippi, and finally in an address delivered in March to the House of Representatives and reprinted as a booklet, Weightman criticized his enemies in the Collins-Smith faction. He focused particular attention on the evils of abolitionism and especially the sins of William Kephart, giving the Ohioan's New Mexico mission considerable publicity both in New Mexico and Washington.

Weightman argued that New Mexicans were not interested in slavery. "The popular feeling," according to his analysis, was "fixed-ly set against that country [New Mexico] being made the area in which to debate" the issue. The territory had already suffered too much by "having our soil made use of by others as a political battlefield," and wanted to avoid that happening again. The blame for raising this vexatious issue rested squarely on the American and Foreign Antislavery Society, a "powerful" organization, its representative, William Kephart of the *Gazette,* and the *National Era* in Washington. They had conspired to "malign" the territorial government, attack the army, and unjustly criticize Governor Calhoun.

Weightman traced Kephart's activities in detail, explaining the dangerous result of his having "broadcast" the "Address" throughout the territory. Chapters were still being reprinted in the *Gazette*. "You will perceive," he wrote Senator Foote, "that . . . unscrupulous persons . . . are urging the law abiding New Mexicans to the commission of treason, and promising assistance they have no right to promise . . . ." The efforts of the abolitionists had been met with nothing but "profound contempt," however. "No excitement took place in New Mexico," he reported, "outside of the immediate family of the editor [Kephart]." The attack became more personal, too. No one, Weightman insisted, could understand the pernicious designs of the *Gazette* "without being introduced to its editor." He characterized Kephart as a trouble-making agent of antislavery interests who had come to New Mexico in the false "garb of a missionary — a minister of the gospel — a man of peace."⁹⁴ He also criticized *Gazette* owner James L. Collins. If he were "as well informed in the simplest principles of law, as he is skillful in the profession of *monte* dealing," Weightman reported sarcastically, he would never have been so critical of Governor Calhoun.⁹⁵

When Kephart heard of Weightman's criticism, he prepared a lengthy rebuttal, apparently sent to the *Missouri Republican*, published in the *Gazette*, and reprinted as a pamphlet entitled *The Editor of the Santa Fe Gazette and Major Weightman, or Truth Vindicated*.⁹⁶ Kephart could not understand the attack, since he had played an inactive part in the recent election. Except for printing a short address by Reynolds and commenting briefly on a letter of Weightman's, the *Gazette* had remained "entirely neutral." Perhaps the delegate-elect was upset over criticism that he had accepted an appointment as Indian Agent for political purposes and to secure free transportation when he had no intention of taking the job. This, in Kephart's view, was dishonest and had deprived the territory of a badly needed agent. Kephart had also denounced "the bare-faced and shameless political profligacy, frauds, and corruption" by which Weightman had been elected. He reiterated the suggestion that neither candidate be seated. These criticisms were mild compared to Kephart's personal attacks in the tract: he condemned the Delegate for his "superlative egotism and self-sufficiency, [which was] only equalled by his moral and intellectual deficiencies." Weightman himself, Kephart continued, was "too insignificant for a serious notice," but since he claimed to be the Delegate from New Mexico, his charges had to be answered.

Kephart was most concerned about the personal attacks on him. Weightman had "seen fit to misrepresent me designedly," the editor claimed, "and from the lowest sinister motives of self aggrandizement." Kephart made no mention of his antislavery connections, but reacted strongly to charges that he had come to New Mexico as a missionary and "entirely abandoned" his calling to go into politics. That, he contended, was "a base falsehood." He had originally been sent on a "mission of observation, with a view of obtaining correct information in relation to facts, [rather] than for establishing a permanent mission." He had preached with Nicholson for a time. Few Americans attended the services; two missionaries were already preaching, and opening a third church would have looked "more like a desire to promulgate sectarianism than pure Christianity." He had been unwilling to continue accepting his salary from the Missionary Assocaition while *"doing nothing,"* and so accepted Collins' offer to edit the *Gazette.* "Had my conscience in such matters been as slack-twisted as Mr. Weightman's, I could have drawn my salary and been content to spend months in doing nothing at other people's expense."[97]

The accusation that he had "scattered broadcast over the Territory" copies of the infamous "Address" was untrue. Only a few had been distributed in Santa Fe before, on the advise of several leading citizens, it had been withdrawn and the remaining copies "boxed up." During the attack on Governor Calhoun's Indian policies, opposition members of the legislature had asked for some of them. "But," Kephart explained, "I saw at a glance the use that was intended to be made of them, and positively refused to let a single one out." Weightman himself had obtained a copy only by the "pitiful strategem" of having Governor Calhoun request one. Such a "gross mistatement of facts" as Weightman had been guilty of was "unpardonable and inexcusable."[98]

Defending Collins against Weightman's charges must have been difficult for Kephart. He himself had written Whipple that the *Gazette's* owner "gambles, drinks his toddy, and sometimes keeps a woman," adding that he was "socially much of a gentleman, honorable as a man of the world, and a man of good judgement and much influence in society."[99] Now he sprang to Collins' defense. While Weightman had been devoting his time in Washington solely to "his own personal affairs," Collins had worked "to get the wants of New Mexico before Congress and have her interests attended to." He had petitioned Congress to secure payment for Mexican volunteers. He had requested an appropriation to open schools.[100] In addition Collins prepared his own "reply to certain slanderous statements" made by Weightman together with "an expose of the duplicity of that gentlemen's course in relation to New Mexico" which Collins and Kephart printed.[101]

These bitter attacks and counterattacks further increased the animosity among New Mexico's politicians. What Kephart thought of Weightman seemingly had little impact in Washington, however, for he was ultimately seated as New Mexico's first delegate.[102]

Judge Crafton Baker

Not only the Catholic clergy, the governor, and the delegate from New Mexico met with Kephart's disapproval. Some of his strongest attacks were aimed at the territorial courts. Like Governors the judges were appointed by the President and confirmed by the Senate. By July, 1851, when the first Chief Justice reached New Mexico, Kephart knew there was "an urgent need" for a court system. The previous "acting judges" serving under the military government had been suspended. Prisoners awaiting trial filled the jails in some areas. Justice had been "thwarted" and county governments bankrupted by the costs of keeping the prisoners.[103]

The first chief justice was unlikely to suit Kephart. Grafton Baker, a Mississippian, had brought a slave with him to New Mexico. Moreover, Baker drank heavily and on at least one occasion had "indulged a bit freely on distilled spirits" before a grand jury session. Later the *Gazette* charged him with "lying in a state of beastly intoxication in one of our lowest doggeries."[104] Kephart quickly concluded that Baker was "incapable of attending to business" and "so notorious" that he ought to make a full confession and promise to reform. A move was initiated to have the judge removed, with Kephart joining others in the circulation of petitions and memorials to be forwarded to Washington.[105] Just before he left Santa Fe to defend himself against these charges, Baker reportedly "got zealous in the temperance cause" and helped organize an abstinence society. Kephart alleged that Baker drank a glass of gin less than a hundred miles out of Santa Fe, however, and predicted he would "have a spree" before reaching Washington.[106]

Ill feeling between Kephart and Baker grew during the judge's absence. Attacks in the *Gazette* became more shrill. "I suppose Judge Baker will [not] relish my *complimentary* notice of him in today's *Gazette*," he wrote Whipple in late November. "He really deserved every lick I gave him, and a good deal more." Should Baker return to New Mexico, which Kephart thought unlikely, he might well challenge the editor to a duel. "If he *should* return and *should* challenge me," Kephart asked sarcastically, "would the Board justify me in fighting him with double barreled howitzers at 1-1/2 miles?"[107]

Just as efforts to unseat Weightman had failed, so too did moves to have Baker removed. Despite what Kephart judged as "the public and notorious" fact of "his disgraceful inebriation during a whole term of court," Baker denied the charges and returned "to the utter astonishment of everyone conversant with the facts." "Does not Baker," Kephart asked "should he return at all, return with his drunkenness endorsed by the Government of the United States? Most assuredly I see no escape from the conclusion."[108]

The Death of Governor Calhoun

Of all his political adversaries, Kephart found James S. Calhoun the most difficult to dislike. The governor had provided Kephart free lodging soon after he reached New Mexico. He had proven to be a kindly, considerate Southern gentleman who sincerely endeavored to improve the territory. Yet, as Kephart became increasingly politically oriented, he and Calhoun became enemies.

The *National Era,* in its issue of February 26, 1852, accused Calhoun of being "no better than an infamous kidnapper." According to the accompanying story, based on an article from the Salt Lake City *Deseret News,* traders with licenses signed by the governor had been authorized "to purchase Indian children, as slaves, for the benefit of persons in New Mexico." The Mormons might be bad, the *Era* screamed, but "they are not so devilish, as to connive at this new trade in human blood. . . ." Study of the original *News* article, however, showed that several companies from New Mexico were trading horses for "Indian Children, firearms, etc." and that one had a license from Calhoun to trade with the Indians. "It does not confirm the statement," Delegate Weightman argued, "that by the license of Governor Calhoun there has been authorized trade of any kind, notwithstanding the reckless and unscrupulous statement of the National Era."[109]

Weightman blamed Kephart for this article, and subsequent historians have often assumed that he was responsible. His guilt is difficult to determine. Kephart's correspondence, upon which most *National Era* articles were based, never raised the issue of Indians being taken captive. No surviving issue of the *Gazette* discusses the issue. April 29, 1852, Kephart noted that "some of the papers in the states" were "down upon Gov. Calhoun pretty severely for his "official kid-napping. I think," Kephart concluded, "he deserves it all."[110]

By then, however, Calhoun's health had deteriorated, probably from cancer, so that even Kephart was reluctant to emphasize the issue. "In his present state of health," Kephart wrote, "I do not think it would be proper or humane to attack him *here,* or even to re-publish the amin-adversions of others."[111] A personal reconciliation between the two men occurred during several friendly meetings. Calhoun assured Kephart that he "had not the slightest unkind feeling" over the *Gazette*'s critical stance toward his adminis-

tration. "We parted on excellent terms."[112] The governor left Santa Fe
early in May, 1852. The hardships of the stagecoach trip were more
than his frail body could stand, however, and he died on the Kansas
plains toward the end of June.[113]

The Missionaries at Loggerheads

John Greiner, a young Ohioan appointed a New Mexico Indian
agent, reached Santa Fe late in July 1851. Kephart liked him, char-
acterizing him as "a genuine Buck-eye — all over Whig, but antislavery withal." "I have no doubt," Kephart thought, "but he will
render a good account of himself."[114] The two men got to know
each other a great deal better, for they shared quarters at Nicholson's home. "I am led to believe that he [Kephart] is under the guidance of the antislavery society," Greiner reported to an Ohio friend,
"and they have been fortunate in their selection of a man who is
resolute, energetic and shrewd."[115]

Greiner was surprised that in New Mexico "everybody and everything" appeared to be "at cross purposes. Even," he reported, "the
missionaries are at loggerheads."[116] What Greiner found was hardly
new, for such animosities, especially between Kephart and Nicholson, on the one hand, and Baptist Hiram Read on the other, had
begun almost as soon as the preachers had met. The disputes had
since been joined by two additional Baptists, Reverend Louis Smith
and Reverend James M. Shaw, who arrived during 1851.[117]

Renewed complaints against Read began when he reported to his
mission board that even though most other religious workers in
New Mexico had met with so little success that they had virtually giv-
en up, his own efforts had been extremely successful. Rather than accept these exaggerations as Read's understandable attempts to prove
the value of his efforts, Kephart joined Nicholson and some of the
other preachers in attacks on Read which were as strongly worded
as any launched against political adversaries. In addition to published criticism in the *Gazette*, he sent letters about Read to various
eastern newspapers and church magazines.

Kephart reported that when he first came to New Mexico, Read
seldom preached, had no Spanish Bibles for distribution, and "had

a greater reputation as a horse jockey than as a preacher." Since then, not more than four or five persons had attended his chapel. What was worse, Read had "done more to compromise the Protestant religion in this field" than anyone else. He cooperated with Catholics, participated in their "Romish processions," and even carried a lighted candle in the funeral march of a priest's concubine. "I believe this community will bear me out in the assertion that in his three years' operations," Kephart argued, "he has scarcely left a visible mark to show his presence in the country, unless it is his brand upon the hips of some horse or mule that has passed through his hands." These were hard things to say about a fellow preacher, Kephart admitted, noting he had long ago "ceased to regard him in that light."[118]

Kephart also challenged Read's claim of having established successful schools in the territory. An editorial published in the *St. Louis Republican* based on an interview with Read credited the Baptist with having founded English schools "such as the Mexican and Pueblo Indians would be willing to send [their children] to and support." The *Gazette* denounced this claim as "simply and unequivocally false." Mexican-Americans and Indians had no intention of sending their youngsters to English language schools, and only Spanish-speaking teachers could hope to succeed. This criticism infuriated Read, who was in the east trying to raise funds to support his mission. He attacked Kephart through the *New York Recorder*. "It is strange," editorialized the paper, "that any inhabitant of New Mexico would be willing to throw an obstacle in the way of so good a work as *founding schools in that territory.*"

This provoked another attack Kephart prepared for submission to the *New York Independent*. Read's primary concern, he now claimed, was to raise money in the East, and he was willing to do anything to accomplish that end. He had visited leading citizens of Santa Fe prior to his departure asking for letters of recommendation. Businessmen eager to increase the amount of money in the city were willing, in Kephart's view, to overlook Read's past failures and dim prospects. "I thought that I could safely say schools were much needed in the territory," John R. Tullis told Kephart, "I thought that if we could get five thousand dollars *thrown out into circulation in our community by the operation* and at the same time stand a chance of doing some things in the way of education, it would be well enough to do so."

The truth, Kephart reported, was that Read's "Santa Fe Academy" never had more than fifteen students. Read's statement that there had been seventy pupils with an average attendance of thirty could not be supported by statistics. *"He has not got them, never had them, and cannot prove them* without forging them." Read had claimed credit for opening a school in Taos, yet the building had been erected by a man who wanted his children educated "without any special reference to the labors of Mr. Read or anyone else." Reverend Shaw's school in Albuquerque had attracted only three students.

Kephart denied his attacks were aimed at retarding the growth of education. "We should rejoice to see school houses dotting this territory like the New England states, or my native Ohio, and the blessings of a liberal education conferred upon every soul." Read, however, was not the kind of schoolman New Mexico needed. "We are not willing to see a sinister man, under the color of benevolence imposing upon the churches . . . . When missionaries get to deceiving the public," he asked, "who then can be trusted?"[119]

As usual Kephart's attacks had little impact on Reverend Read. By August 1852 the Baptist had returned to Santa Fe and was once again acting like "the biggest dog in the boneyard." He had collected several thousand dollars in the East, which he planned to use for building a chapel or opening schools. Soon he transferred to Albuquerque, as Kephart described it, "rolling in his carriage with five span of horses, his wife diddling on a costly piano, boasting that he has *five thousand dollars in his possession,* writing lying reports for the newspapers in the States, and doing nothing."[120]

The Costs of a New Mexico Mission

During 1852 the American Missionary Association and American and Foreign Antislavery Society became increasingly concerned about the growing cost of Kephart's mission. The two groups had originally agreed to pay the Ohio preacher's "living expenses," presumably including travel, housing, clothing, food, and the like. In January 1851, for example, when Kephart filed his first quarterly report, expenses included a coat, a Spanish dictionary, books, a thermometer, repair of a watch, candles, and other small items. His bill from July 5, 1850, to January 1, 1851, had totaled $800.[121]

Kephart's charges increased dramatically after he assumed the editorship of the *Gazette*. While he had initially predicted the paper would break even or make a profit, it lost money regularly. Kephart had agreed, without the approval of his sponsors, to make up a share of any losses. Moreover, the absence of Collins in the east left him responsible for paying employees, purchasing supplies, and so on. Kephart assumed that such costs were part of his legitimate living expenses since they were less than would have been needed to start a purely abolitionist paper.[122]

The system used to obtain money caused further problems. It was too dangerous to carry large amounts of cash across the plains; no telegraph yet connected Santa Fe with the States; and personal checks were seldom used. At first Kephart cashed drafts on New York and Philadelphia banks given him by Whipple or Tappan. They could be redeemed in Santa Fe at a slight discount. Once his initial fund was exhausted, however, Kephart began the questionable practice of writing "orders on the associations" whenever he needed money without prior authorization.[123]

Kephart's financial woes worsened as a result of what he presumed to have been a robbery. Just prior to leaving for the east, Collins had cashed a $500 order, the proceeds of which Kephart put in a trunk in his bedroom at the Nicholson's. Several weeks later, after some money had been removed to pay expenses, he discovered that the lock had been forced, and the remaining money was gone. Two Mexican-American boys who had slept in the room were presumably the culprits, although no real evidence could be found, and Kephart's books were so poorly kept that he could only guess how much money had been taken. "I believe that from the tallest rico down to the lowest 'greaser,' man, woman, and child," Kephart insisted with typical prejudiced exaggeration, "these Mexicans will steal . . . . We have to watch them like hawks. . . ."[124]

Kephart was too busy printing the legislative journals to submit his quarterly expenditures report in April 1852. The personal expense list he finally submitted at midyear totalled $686.32, including a large boarding bill from Nicholson, the $115 "stolen" from his trunk, and $150 for round-trip stage fare to Independence to pick up the new type for the *Gazette*. To pay *Gazette* expenses, however, he had already drawn $600 on the association and expected to write a draft for $1,000 more within a few days.[125] With the printing office costing $100 a week while the journals were being printed, late in July he wrote still another $500 draft.[126]

As expenses grew, Kephart became apprehensive at receiving no letters from Whipple. "*Why don't some of you write me?*" he asked plaintively in late August 1852. "If you have something against me, say so — I have never shunned to meet my responsibilities. If you say nothing, then surely a word of encouragement amid multiplied assaults upon every hand might impart some degree of courage to a flagging spirit." Eight months without a single word "either of rebuke or love — encouragement or instruction — is enough to crush anyone without any other weight."[127]

Three letters received in the September mail stunned the usually optimistic abolitionist. He wrote Whipple that they had "given me much heart-pain — more than all things else" since coming to New Mexico. "I can bear the wrath of my enemies and repel it," he moaned, "so long as I am conscious *I have the confidence of my brethren.*" When that wavered, though, the will to persist diminished. He tried to explain the need for so much additional money: Collins' extended absence in the states, increased costs, the inability to collect bills. Kepharts argued that his only alternatives had been to write the unauthorized drafts or to close the *Gazette* and abandon any possible profit. "My heavenly Father is judge that it was not in wantonness that I drew upon you," he pleaded, "but from necessity as painful to myself as it could have been to others." Whatever the final judgement, Kephart knew that he had "labored with uneasing toil night and day."[128] Two major drafts which the association refused to pay were eventually made up with money the *Gazette* received for territorial printing,[129] but the associations had obviously lost confidence in their New Mexico representative.

The End of the Mission

Kephart was aware by late 1852 that his mission in New Mexico was rapidly coming to an end. His original preaching and anti-slavery activities had largely been supplanted by newspaper work and political wrangling. His eastern sponsors had objected to his high expenses and his practice of drawing money without prior approval. Moreover, concern about the spread of slavery to New Mexico diminished as attention focused increasingly on Kansas. After 1854, when passage of the Kansas-Nebraska Act extended the squatter-sovereignty principal to new territories, abolitionists turned their attention there.

In May 1852 Kephart first reported his plan to visit home and asked if the committee would want him to return. He thought it was important to maintain an antislavery presence in the Southwest. "The Territory is ours *now*," he reported "and we must *make the best we can of it*, or abandon it altogether." Kephart was determined, if he came back, to bring a wife. His argument that it was "*dangerous* for *any man* to live" in New Mexico unmarried raises the suspicion that he himself may have been tempted by the immorality which he constantly denounced. He also hoped to open a church of his own rather than cooperate with others and to begin his own paper instead of editing the *Gazette*. All this would produce "a considerable increase in cost."[130]

Kephart knew by late in the year, having been rebuked for his heavy expenditures, that such an expensive proposal was unlikely to be accepted. The critical illness of a sister further encouraged his prompt return to the States. Nicholson, who had left for the States the previous spring, would not be returning either. Kephart learned in November that the Methodists had decided to "abandon the field, at least for the present" and asked him to dispose of their property.[131]

Arrangements to reorganize the *Gazette* proceeded swiftly after Collins' return late in 1852. During the fall, printer William Drew took over the publishing responsibilities.[132] The issue of January 29,

1853, announced that he was joining the Collins-Kephart partnership and assured readers that the new arrangement would "place the paper on a secure and permanent basis for the future." The same issue reported that Kephart would be leaving for the States with the next mail and would not be back "for several months to come." His name remained on the masthead, however, until late spring.[133]

Kephart's accompanying letter "to our readers" strongly suggested that his leave-taking was permanent. He thanked friends for their personal kindness and editorial indulgence. His editorial excesses were defended with arguments that the good of the territory not personal gain had always motivated him. He especially urged Mexican-Americans to remember that New Mexico would be populated by Americans and foreigners and that its destiny was tied inseparably with the United States. In order to prosper, the territory's citizens "must think and act more for themselves," Kephart argued, "and be less ready to follow the lead of scheming and designing political demagogues." Education being absolutely vital, Kephart urged federal support to start up a school system. Needed money might already have been appropriated, he insisted in a partisan attack, had someone other than Weightman been elected Delegate. What New Mexico needed was a man who understood the territory and its needs, who expected to make it his home, and who had "the dignity of character" to earn him respect in Washington.[134]

Kephart left Santa Fe with the February 1853 mail and traveled to Washington and New York for meetings with his sponsors before returning to Ohio. The results of these conferences confirmed his fears. The American Missionary Association's board declined to pay Kephart's share of *Gazette* losses and decided to close its mission in the Southwest. Kephart was disappointed but accepted the inevitable. "I can easily conceive many reasons," he wrote Whipple, "why Providence should not send *me* back to that field, not the least of which is my own unfaithfulness and inefficiency in the time past." He hoped that New Mexico would not be forgotten. "In my heart I cannot relinquish the hope that some Christian, antislavery man be found willing to stand in the breach between New Mexico and the slave-power."[135]

REFERENCES

1   Charles W. Ramsdell, "The Natural Limits of Slavery Expansion," *Mississippi Valley Historical Review*, XXVI (1929), pp. 151-71. Charles D. Hart, "Slavery Expansion in the Territories, 1850," *New Mexico Historical Review*, XLI (1966), pp. 269-86.

2   Clifton H. Johnson, "The American Missionary Association, 1846-1861, A Study of Christian Abolitionism," unpublished doctoral dissertation, The University of North Carolina, 1958.

3   George Whipple to Arthur Tappan, February 28, 1850, American Missionary Association Archives, Dillard University, New Orleans, Louisiana. (Hereinafter cited as AMAA).

4   For conflicting dates, see *The Herald and Presbyter*, June 20, 1894, p. 16, and Minutes, Synod of South Dakota, 1894. The author is grateful to Gerald W. Gillette, Presbyterian Historical Society, Philadelphia, for this information.

5   Henry Howe, *Historical Collections of Ohio* (Cincinnati: Robert Clarke and Co., 1875), p. 71; Wilbur H. Siebert, "A Quaker Section of the Underground Railroad in Northern Ohio," *Ohio State Archaeological and Historical Quarterly,"* XXXIX (1930), pp. 491-93.

6   Dwight L. Dumond, *Antislavery: The Crusade for Freedom in America* (Ann Arbor: University of Michigan Press, 1961), pp. 134-36; Paul R. Grim, "The Rev. John Rankin, Early Abolitionist," *Ohio State Archaeological and Historical Quarterly*, XLVI, (1937), pp. 215-52.

7   Andrew E. Murray, *Presbyterians and the Negro — A History* (Philadelphia: Presbyterian Historical Society, 1966), pp. 119-22.

8   *Annual Report of the American Missionary Association, 1850*, p. 36, quoted in Johnson, "American Missionary Association," pp. 492-93.

9   One letter appeared in the *Arkansas Gazette and Democrat*, while others have been quoted from other sources throughout the United States.

10   *The History of Brown County, Ohio* (Chicago: W. H. Beers and Co., 1883), biographical section, pp. 56-57.

11   Kephart to Whipple, July 28 and August 29, 1951, AMAA.

12   Johnson, "American Missionary Association," p. 492.

13   *Santa Fe Weekly Gazette*, January 29, 1853, pp. 2-3.

14   *Santa Fe Weekly Gazette*, March 12, April 9, April 30, May 7, May 21, May 28, all p. 2, contain letters from Kephart describing his journey.

15   Johnson, "American Missionary Association," p. 494.

16   Kephart's letters, *Santa Fe Weekly Gazette*, May 28, June 2, June 11, 1853. pp. 2-3.

17   *Santa Fe Weekly Gazette*, November 26, 1853, p. 2.

18   E. B. Welsh, "Notes and Extracts" on the history of the Free Presbyterian Church, Synod of Ohio Historical Collection, College of Wooster, Ohio.

19   *The Herald and Presbyter*, June 20, 1894, p. 16.

20   Ibid; Minutes, Synod of South Dakota, 1894, Presbyterian Historical Society.

21 David Meriwether, *My Life in the Mountains and on the Plains.*, ed., Robert A. Griffen (Norman: University of Oklahoma Press, 1965), and George A. McCall, *New Mexico in 1850: A Military View,* ed., Robert W. Frazer (Norman: University of Oklahoma Press, 1968).

22 For a survey of the literature, see Jack D. Rittenhouse, *The Santa Fe Trail: A Historical Bibliography* (Albuquerque: University of New Mexico Press, 1971).

23 *The National Era,* September 26, 1850, p. 3.

24 *New York Daily Tribune,* May 29, 1850, quoted in Louise Barry, *The Beginning of the West* (Topeka: Kansas State Historical Society, 1972), p. 936.

26 Ibid., pp. 956, 968.

26 Morris F. Taylor, *First Mail West: Stagecoach Lines on the Santa Fe Trail* (Albuquerque: University of New Mexico Press, 1971), p. 13.

27 Barry, *Beginning of the West,* pp. 957-64.

28 *The National Era,* September 26, 1850, p. 3.

29 Ibid., October 10, 1850, p. 3.

30 Ibid.

31 Ibid.; *The National Era,* October 31, 1850, p. 3.

32 Barry, *Beginning of the West,* pp. 950, 962.

33 *The National Era,* October 31, 1850, p. 3.

34 Ibid.

35 Kephart to Whipple, November 19, 1850, AMAA.

36 Ibid., and *The National Era,* January 23, 1851, p. 1.

37 Kephart to Whipple, November 19, 1850, AMAA.

38 Ibid., and *The National Era,* January 23, 1851, p. 1.

39 Ibid.

40 Kephart to Whipple, November 19, 1850, AMAA.

41 *The National Era,* January 23, 1851, p. 1.

42 Colin B. Goodykoontz, *Home Missions on the American Frontier* (Caldwell, Idaho: The Caxton Printers, 1939), pp. 271-82.

43 Kephart to Whipple, November 19, 1850, AMAA.

44 Goodykoontz, *Home Missions,* p. 325; Barry, *Beginning of the West,* p. 970.

45 Kephart to Whipple, November 19, 1850, AMAA.

46 For a full discussion of anti-Catholic literature, see Ray A. Billington, *The Protestant Crusade, 1800-1860* (New York: The Macmillan Co., 1938), pp. 253, 345 ff.

47 Kephart to Whipple, February 10, 1851, AMAA.

48 Ralph E. Twitchell, *Leading Facts of New Mexican History* (Cedar Rapids, Iowa: The Torch Press, 1912), II, p. 138.

49 Kephart to Whipple, January 25, 1851, January 28, 1851, AMAA.

50 "P.S. Jan. 30," appended to Kephart to Whipple, January 28, 1851, AMAA.

51 Dumas Malone, ed., *Dictionary of American Biography* (New York: Charles Scribner's Sons, 1953), X, pp. 11-12.

52 William Jay, "Address to the Inhabitants of New Mexico and California, on the Omission by Congress to Provide Them with Territorial Governments, and on the Social and Political Evils of Slavery" (New York: American and Foreign Anti-slavery Society, 1849), 56 pp.

53 Kephart to Whipple, December 31, 1850, January 25, 1851, AMAA.

54 Kephart to Whipple February 10, 1851, AMAA.

55 Kephart to Whipple, February 20, 1851, AMAA. *The National Era*, April 7, 1851, p. 2.

56 Harvey L. Carter, *"Dear Old Kit": The Historical Christopher Carson* (Norman: University of Oklahoma Press, 1968), pp. 3-12.

57 *The National Era*, April 3, 1851, p. 3. Quoting a reprint of this article in the *Arkansas Gazette and Democrat*, Harvey L. Carter used the description of Hatcher in his sketch in Leroy Hafen, ed. *The Mountain Men and the Fur Trade of the Far West* (Glendale: Arthur H. Clark Co., 1966), vol. IV, p. 136. No biographer of Carson has made use of this description.

58 Robert V. Hine, *Bartlett's West* (New Haven: Yale University Press, 1968), p. 30.

59 *The National Era*, April 17, 1851, p. 2.

60 "P.S." March 27, 1851, appended to Kephart to Whipple, March 26, 1851, AMAA.

61 *The National Era*, October 2, 1851, p. 3. Compare with Paul Horgan, *Lamy of Santa Fe* (New York: Farrar, Straus, and Giroux, 1975), pp. 208-10.

62 Calvin Horn, *New Mexico's Troubled Years* (Albuquerque: Horn and Wallace, 1963), pp. 21-23.

63 *The National Era*, April 17, 1851, p. 2.

64 Horn, *New Mexico's Troubled Years*, p. 21.

65 *The National Era*, April 17, 1851, p .2.

66 Ibid.

67 *The National Era*, May 8, 1851, p. 3.

68 Kephart to Whipple, December 31, 1850, AMAA.

69 Douglas C. McMurtrie, "Notes from Manuscript," in Jackson E. Towne, "Printing in New Mexico Beyond Santa Fe and Taos, 1848-1875," *New Mexico Historical Review*, 35, No. 2 (April 1960), pp. 112-14. Also Porter A. Stratton, *The Territorial Press of New Mexico, 1834-1912* (Albuquerque: University of New Mexico Press, 1969), pp. 2-3; and Pearce S. Grove, Becky J. Barnett, and Sandra J. Hansen, *New Mexico Newspapers* (Albuquerque: University of New Mexico Press, 1975), pp. 475, 480.

70 McMurtrie, "Notes," p. 115. Grove, Barnett, and Hansen, *New Mexico Newspapers*, p. 470 dates the *Gazette* from April 26, 1851; and Stratton, *Territorial Press*, p. 3, from June 1851. Both are probably too late. Kephart's reports suggest that it had been published intermittently since late the previous year. Loomis M. Ganaway, *New Mexico and the Sectional Controversy* (Albuquerque: University of New Mexico Press, 1944), p. 54, n. 66 cites an issue (now missing) for "December 7 [?], 1850."

71 "P.S." April 28, 1851, attached to Kephart to Whipple, April 22, 1851, AMAA.

72   Kephart to Whipple, June 27, 1851, and September 30, 1851, AAMA.

73   Historical Records Survey, *Checklist of New Mexico Imprints and Publications, 1784-86, American Imprints Inventory,* No. 25 (Michigan Historical Records Survey, 1942, repr. New York: Kraus Reprints, 1964), p. 25. Wilma Loy Shelton, *Checklist of New Mexico Publications* (Albuquerque: University of New Mexico Press, 1954), p. 143, incorrectly lists the publisher as Collins and "Kephard."

74   For a general discussion, see Stratton, *Territorial Press,* pp. 15 ff.

75   Kephart to Whipple, November 29, 1851, AMAA.

76   Ibid., January 28, 1852, AMAA.

77   Ibid., April 2 & 9, 1852, AMAA.

78   Ibid., July 31, 1852, AMAA.

79   Ibid., May 16, 1851, AMAA.

80   Twitchell, *Leading Facts,* II, p. 352. The name is misspelled "Kephardt."

81   Howard R. Lamar, *The Far Southwest, 1846-1912* (New Haven: Yale University Press, 1966), pp. 75-82; Robert W. Larson, *New Mexico's Quest for Statehood, 1846-1912* (Albuquerque: University of New Mexico Press, 1968), pp. 25-64.

82   Kephart to Whipple, May 16, 1851, AMAA.

83   Ibid., June 27, 1851, AMAA.

84   Earl S. Pomeroy, *The Territories and the United States, 1861-1890* (Philadelphia: University of Pennsylvania Press, 1947), pp. 3 ff.

85   "P.S." April 23, 1851, attached to Kephart to Whipple, April 22, 1851, AMAA. *The National Era,* June 22, 1851, p. 3.

86   Kephart to Whipple, May 16, 1851, and *The National Era,* July 17, 1851, p. 3.

87   Kephart to Whipple, May 16, 1851, AMAA.

88   *The National Era,* July 17, 1851, p. 3.

89   Ibid., September 11, 1851, p. 2.

90   Ganaway, *New Mexico and the Sectional Controversy,* p. 55.

91   Historical Records Survey, *Check List,* pp. 25, 27.

92   *The National Era,* October 2, 1851, p. 3; and Kephart to Tappan, August 28, 1851, AMAA.

93   *The National Era,* November 13, 1851, p. 2. For details on the election, see Larson, *New Mexico's Quest,* pp. 66 ff.

94   Kephart "to the People of New Mexico," August 25, 1852, AMAA; and *The Congressional Globe,* 32nd Cong., 1st Sess., March 15, 1852, pp. 754-56.

95   Quoted in Kephart, *The Editor of the Santa Fe Gazette and Major Weightman or Truth Vindicated* (Santa Fe: Gazette Office, 1852), 8 pp.

96   Ibid., and Kephart "to the People," August 25, 1852, AMAA.

97   Ibid.

98   Kephart, *The Editor,* pp. 4-5.

99   Kephart to Whipple, August 9, 1851, AMAA.

100   Kephart "to the People," August 25, 1852, AMAA.

101   Historical Records Survey, *Check List,* p. 28; *Santa Fe Weekly Gazette,* Nov. 27, 1852; Jan. 22, 1853, p. 2.

102   Kephart to Whipple, June 26, 1852, AMAA.

103   *The National Era,* September 11, 1851, p. 2.

104   Arie W. Poldervaart, *Black-Robed Justice* (Santa Fe: Historical Society of New Mexico, 1948), pp. 38-39.

105   *The National Era,* November 13, 1851, p. 3.

106   Kephart to Whipple, September 30, 1851, AMAA, and *The National Era,* December 18, 1851, p. 3.

107   Kephart to Whipple, November 29, 1851, AMAA.

108   "P.S." June 30, attached to Kephart to Whipple, June 26, 1852, AMAA.

109   *Congressional Globe,* 32nd Cong., 1st Sess., March 15, 1852, p. 754.

110   Kephart to Whipple, April 28, 1852, AMAA.

111   Ibid.

112   Kephart to Whipple, May 7, 1852, AMAA.

113   Barry, *Beginning of the West,* p. 1107.

114   Kephart to Whipple, July 24, 1851, and "P.S." July 25, 1851, AMAA.

115   Greiner's letter of July 29, 1851, in Tod G. Galloway, ed., "Private Letters of a Government Official in the Southwest," *Journal of American History,* 3 (1909), p. 546.

116   Ibid.

117   Barry, *Beginning of the West,* pp. 999-1000, 1046.

118   Kephart to Whipple, September 30, 1851, AMAA.

119   Kephart to the "Editors of the Independent," May 29, 1852, AMAA.

120   Kephart to Whipple, August 30, 1852, and November 28, 1852, AMAA.

121   Ibid., January 25, 1851, AMAA.

122   Ibid., April 22, June 27, 1851, AMAA.

123   Ibid., January 24, June 27, September 30, 1851, AMAA.

124   Ibid., December 29, 1851, AMAA.

125   Ibid., June 26, 1852, AMAA.

126   Ibid., July 31, 1852, AMAA.

127   Ibid., August 30, 1852, AMAA.

128   Ibid., September 27, 1852, AMAA.

129   Ibid., December 29, 1852, AMAA.

130   Ibid., May 7, 1852, AMAA.

131   Ibid., November 28, 1852, AMAA.

132   *Santa Fe Weekly Gazette,* November 13, 1852, p. 2

133   Ibid., January 29, 1853, p. 2. Ganaway, *New Mexico and the Sectional Controversy,* p. 58 is incorrect in stating that Collins "dismissed" Kephart. Collins edited the paper for a short time before W. W. H. Davis assumed the editor's chair.

134   Ibid., pp. 2-3.

135   Kephart to Whipple, May 18, June 30, 1853, AMAA.

John T. Rankin, his wife, and ten children.